Encyclopedia Brown's
Book of Wacky
SPIES

DONALD J. SOBOL

Encyclopedia Brown's Book of Wacky
SPIES

Illustrated by Ted Enik

WILLIAM MORROW AND COMPANY
New York • 1984

1   2   3   4   5   6   7   8   9   10

Library of Congress Cataloging in Publication Data
Sobol, Donald J., 1924– Encyclopedia Brown's book of wacky spies.
Summary: Briefly describes undercover activities of spies from various
historical periods and geographical areas.
1. Espionage—Juvenile literature. 2. Spies—Juvenile literature. [1.
Espionage. 2. Spies] I. Enik, Ted, ill. II. Title.
UB270.5.S6   1984   327.1'2   83–17179
ISBN 0–688–02744–X

For Jay Mallin

Key to Symbols

American
Revolution

Civil War

World War I

World War II

all other times

Contents

Encyclopedia Brown's
Book of Wacky
SPIES

Introduction

Although Encyclopedia Brown was only ten, he had never run up against a mystery that he could not solve.

During the winter he helped his father, the police chief of Idaville. After school let out for the summer, he opened his own detective agency in the garage. He wanted to help the children of the neighborhood, too.

On Friday, Mitzie Klunkmann came into the Brown Detective Agency. "Someone is spying on me!" she blurted. "I want you to find out who it is!"

"Why should someone spy on you?" Encyclopedia asked.

"Because the Idaville cook-off is tomorrow," Mitzie answered. "Every kid entered is dying to get his hands on my worm-cookie recipe."

"Who would want to steal a worm-cookie recipe?"

"Farnsworth Grant," snapped Mitzie. "He won the cook-off last year with sourdough bagels. This year he'll enter a recipe for chopped chicken liver. He knows my worms can beat his liver. If he gets hold of my recipe, he can claim I stole it from him!"

Encyclopedia realized that Mitzie was so worked up over the cook-off that she was seeing things. He said, "Farnsworth has been visiting his aunt in Glenn City all week. He can't be spying on you." As he spoke, the detective was thinking that a worm cookie couldn't win a prize at a dead-bait contest.

"Farnsworth Grant probably lied to you about visiting his aunt," Mitzie said. "Oh, why did I come here! What do you know about spies?"

"A few things," murmured Encyclopedia.

"Name one spy!" Mitzie challenged.

"Nathan Hale," said Encyclopedia.

"*Everyone* knows about *him*," Mitzie scoffed. "He was the spy in the Revolution who said, 'I only regret that I have but one life to give for my country.' "

"Lose," Encyclopedia corrected. "He said, 'I only regret that I have but one life to *lose* for my country.' "

"Where'd you learn that?" demanded Mitzie.

"Where'd you learn that Farnsworth Grant is going to enter a chopped liver recipe at the cook-off?" the detective inquired evenly.

Mitzie lowered her head. "I did a little spying myself," she confessed.

Now wasn't the time for criticism. Mitzie wasn't herself. She needed to be calmed down.

3

"I've been gathering true stories about spies," Encyclopedia said. "Would you like to see them?"

Encyclopedia walked to the shelves on the wall and took down a large red scrapbook. He laid it on the battered table that he used for an office desk.

"A good spy is worth a general," he said.

Mitzie turned to the first page. "I'm sorry I accused Farnsworth Grant," she apologized. "I guess I'm the suspicious type, and I got carried away."

Her voice trailed off. She had begun to read . . . .

1
Foolish Spies

Say that again? Carl Hans Lody, a German spy in England, heard incredible rumors: Russian troops were traveling through England on the way to the fighting in France. The rumors stemmed from eyewitness accounts of troop trains chugging along with window blinds pulled down.

Actually, the trains carried Scottish soldiers. The blinds were pulled because the soldiers were sleeping. When asked where they were from, the Scots replied, "Ross-shire," which sounded like "Russia."

Lody wired Germany of the presence of "Russian" troops in England. Startled by the news, the Germans held back two divisions from the front to meet this "Russian" threat. As a result, they lost the momentous Battle of the Marne.

And Lody won the title of "the spy who lost the war."

The wurst that could happen. Two German spies sneaked into England by sea. They were caught when a shore patrol found them sitting on the beach eating German sausages for breakfast.

Out on a limb. Once upon a time there was a tree that caught a spy.

The year was 1939. The scene: the second floor of a police station in Japan.

Miyagi Yotoku was being questioned. He remained expressionless, his lips sealed against admitting to the charge of spying for Russia. Rather than reveal the names of other members of his ring, he attempted suicide by hurling himself out the window.

He wasn't killed. He landed in a tree and broke his leg.

The lesson learned: It takes more than heroics to be a hero. The next day Yotoku confessed from his hospital bed and named the ring members.

Caught by the camera. Lafayette Baker passed himself off as a traveling photographer. He roamed through Confederate units gathering data for the Union.

Eventually suspicion developed when nothing else did. Baker was arrested; he seemed to be taking photographs, but he never produced any.

He couldn't. His camera was broken.

Smoke screen. Two spies for Germany were in Portsmouth, England, posing as cigar importers. In their cables, quantities of cigars referred to British warships. They were imprisoned after ordering 48,000 cigars in 10 days—enough stogies to last the cigar smokers of Portsmouth indefinitely.

Taken to the cleaners. Mikhail Gorin was a Russian tourist representative who tripped up because he let his pockets do the traveling.

One day in late 1938, a dry cleaner's truck stopped at his Los Angeles home. Gorin sent off a suit, but forgot to check the pockets. In the pocket of his coat the driver found a $50 bill and several sheets of notes concerning the Japanese spies on the West Coast.

Station break. Heinrich Albert took a snooze and awoke the public to German undercover activity in the United States.

It was 3 P.M., July 25, 1915, less than two years before America entered the war. In New York City, Albert, an official at the German embassy, boarded a Seventh Avenue subway train at Rector Street. With him was George Viereck, an American propaganda expert who worked for the Germans.

At the 23rd Street station Viereck got off. With no one to talk to, Albert leaned back in his seat, closed his eyes, and dozed off. The noise of the car doors opening at the 50th Street station roused him with a start. He jumped up and hurried out, leaving behind his briefcase.

Frank Burke, a secret service agent who had been trailing Albert, immediately snatched up the briefcase. It contained papers detailing widespread German plots against U.S. arms' factories. The New York *World* published the sensational documents, and Americans from coast to coast were alerted to the German menace.

9

Heinrich Albert became a household name overnight. His snooze of the century brought him fame as the "Minister without Portfolio."

Scooped. William Heron holds the record for useless information.

Heron got wind—no doubt a tail wind—of an American plot to kidnap the British commander-in-chief, Sir Henry Clinton. He warned the authorities, raising eyebrows hither and yon.

The kidnapping had been attempted, and had failed, on December 24, 1780—five weeks before Heron's warning.

Simple Simon. Dressed as a Norwegian seaman, the veteran German spy Walter Simon landed at Dingle Bay, Ireland. He hiked directly to the railroad station where he shared the platform with three men who were waiting for a train.

"When does the next train leave for Dublin, mates?" Simon inquired.

The three men turned and stared at him strangely. One of them finally said, "You missed it. The last train to Dublin left here fourteen years ago."

Within hours, Walter Simon was sitting in a cell in the police station in Tralee, his spy career permanently derailed.

Knock, knock. Karl Meir and Rudolph Waldberg rowed ashore on the southeastern coast of England.

The next morning at a little after nine o'clock, Meir rapped on the door of a pub in Lydd and asked for a bottle of cider. First mistake, last mistake. His instructors in Germany had failed to teach him that English pubs didn't legally open until after ten. He was told to come back later. He did, and was welcomed by the police.

Waldberg, left on his own, lasted 24 hours longer, a remarkable feat considering his handicap. He couldn't speak English.

Identity crisis. Hamilton Ballentine, a British colonel, was returning to his lines during the siege of Charleston. He ran into a soldier who he thought was from his own army.

Ballentine gave his name. The soldier, on picket duty, said that wasn't good enough. Anyone can make up a name.

Hell's bells! The indignant Ballentine whipped out plans of the American defense works that he was smuggling back to the British. Was *that* good enough?

That was good enough.

The soldier turned out to be an American. He lost no time making a prisoner of the hot-tempered British colonel whose blunder had blown his cover.

Eeney, meeney, money. The English currency system, so confusing to foreigners, betrayed a spy who was trying to buy a railroad ticket.

The clerk told him the price of his ticket was "ten and six," meaning 10 shillings and sixpence. Without hesitation, the spy counted out 10 pounds and 6 shillings, more than 18 times the fare.

Be it ever so bumbled. The Israelis sought to place a spy in Egypt. This agent would play the part of the consul general from El Salvador, a tiny country in faraway Central America. The agent selected spoke fluent Spanish and knew Central America like the palm of his hand.

The Egyptians were advised that the "consul general" would be traveling in Europe. Well dressed and looking like a rich Latin American, the Israeli arrived at the Egyptian embassy in Brussels, Belgium. After a friendly conversation with the Egyptian consul, he was asked to fill out some diplomatic forms.

The Egyptian asked the Israeli where he was born.

"Haifa," the Israeli responded without thinking. Haifa is a city in Israel, not El Salvador.

With that, the elaborate plan to get an agent into Egypt collapsed.

With spies like these, who needs the enemy? In 1066 King Harold of England, having already defeated a Norwegian army of invaders, hastened south to battle a second and larger host, the Normans under Duke William.

Harold halted some seven miles to the northwest of Duke William's fortified camps. He dispatched spies to scout the enemy.

The spies returned with astounding news. There were probably more clergymen in the Norman camps than soldiers in Harold's army. Had Duke William brought legions of priests across the channel to chant masses?

No leader had ever listened to so bubble-headed an outpouring of wrong information. But Harold was not misled. Unlike his spies, he knew the Norman fashion.

The English let their hair and mustaches grow long, whereas the Normans cropped their hair and shaved their upper lips—as did the clergy in England. The Norman "priests" were men-at-arms.

Dressed to kill. Karl Richter parachuted into England and was quickly apprehended. He claimed he was just out for a walk. But at the police station, where he was searched, his alibi got mussed. For a fellow with no place to go, he was incriminatingly overdressed—he had on two pairs of socks and three pairs of underwear.

Johanns-come-lately. After lengthy training in Germany, William Colepaugh and Eric Gimpel were transported across the Atlantic by submarine. A rubber boat put them ashore on the coast of Maine.

Using aliases, the two made their way to Bangor and traveled by train to New York. Everything went smoothly.

Smoothly if not quickly.

Their principal assignment was to ascertain the effect of German propaganda on the 1944 presidential election campaign. When at last Colepaugh and Gimpel were settled in New York City, the election was over.

Ooops. Charles Albert Van den Kieboon and Sjord Pons, Dutchmen who had gone over to the Germans, beached their boat in England late at night. Their shoes weren't dry before they were taken prisoner.

In the darkness they had landed smack by an encampment of the Somerset Light Infantry.

Oh, shoot. American torpedoes in the early years of the war were often faulty. German torpedoes suffered from the same faults.

The strangely similar problems pointed to something beyond coincidence. Apparently German spies at the Newport Torpedo Station in the United States had stolen the torpedo designs without knowing that they were flawed.

16

End of the line. Vera Erickson, Werner Waelti, and Karl Drueke were flown into Scotland by seaplane. The sun had not yet risen, and in the gloom the spies tried to get their bearings. To find out exactly where they were, they trudged along railroad tracks to the nearest station.

It was early in the war, 1940, and German intelligence suffered from gaps in its knowledge of life in wartime Britain. The spies did not know that all station names had been taken down as a security measure.

Erickson, who spoke the best English, went up to a railroad worker. Foolishly she asked him, "Can you tell us where we are?"

The railroad worker smelled something fishy. Only people foreign to the area wouldn't know where they were. And foreigners traveling before dawn . . .

"Port Gordon," he replied, and immediately afterward told the police.

The three spies soon knew where they stood with the Scots—in jail.

Dusted off. Stig Wennerström, a lieutenant colonel in the Swedish Army, spied for the Russians for more than 10 years. He was finally forced to come clean —by a housemaid. While dusting in his attic, she uncovered films of secret documents, which she turned over to the authorities.

Photo finish. Oleg Penkovskiy, a colonel in the Russian intelligence services, was a double agent. He spied for his country and for the Americans and British.

When Russian spy catchers finally closed in, he was the picture of guilt. Found in his apartment were photographs of him taken during a trip to London. Penkovskiy had proudly posed for them, wearing British and American army uniforms.

Great Scott. The Union captain stalked back and forth, glowering at the man he had arrested. The man was barefoot and drenched from the heavy rain.

"What is your name?"

"E.J. Allen," the prisoner repeated for the third time.

"What is your business?"

"I have nothing more to say." The man had previously claimed that he had become lost in the rainstorm in downtown Washington, D.C.

The captain stiffened with impatience. He seemed tempted to snatch up a pistol on the desk in front of him. Instead, he turned to a sergeant and instructed him to march the prisoner to the guardhouse.

Early the next morning the prisoner bribed a guard to deliver a message to Colonel Thomas A. Scott, assistant secretary of war. Within the hour the captain and the prisoner were summoned to Scott's home.

Scott directed the officer to release his prisoner and led the man into another room. The captain was requested to join them a few minutes later. Asked to explain the arrest, the captain said he had been visiting a friend, and upon returning he noticed the man following him. He'd had him arrested.

Scott asked, "Last evening, captain, did you see anyone who is unfriendly to the government?"

"No, sir, I have seen no one of that character."

"Are you positive?"

"I am, sir."

"Captain," said Scott, "you may consider yourself under arrest."

The friend upon whom the captain had been calling was a Confederate spy, Rose Greenhow. When the captain's quarters were searched, further proof was found that he had been leaking information to the enemy.

"E.J. Allen" was actually Allan Pinkerton. The captain, a Confederate spy, had made the mistake of arresting the head of the Union secret service!

How green was my valet. The cost was high, but the goods would be worth it.

A man showed up at the German embassy in Ankara, Turkey, offering to sell top-secret British documents for 20,000 English pounds. The Germans agreed to the deal, and the man turned over the documents, which included a report on the recent conference of Allied leaders at Teheran, Iran.

The man who sold the documents boasted ideal credentials. He was the valet to the British ambassador in Turkey. Still, the documents seemed *too* good. The Germans distrusted them.

The valet should have distrusted the Germans. They paid him with counterfeit money.

An explosive situation. Klaus Fuchs, a British scientist, was being questioned by a security investigator in England in 1950. Suddenly Fuchs clammed up. He refused to discuss details of the atomic bomb's construction—the same details he was suspected of having sold to the Russians.

The investigator, Fuchs pointed out, lacked security clearance for such top-secret information.

2
Successful Spies

🔎 **I've got a secret.** James Rivington and Robert Townsend became partners in a coffeehouse in New York in 1779. Both pretended to be loyal to the king. In fact, both were secret agents for General George Washington—agents so secret that neither knew the other was a spy.

🔎 **Shhh!** Sir George Downing, Britain's envoy to Holland in the seventeenth century, justly bragged about the spies in his service.

One night a couple of his light-fingered agents stole into the bedroom of John de Witt, Grand Pensionary of Holland. While de Witt snored like a foghorn, the spies filched the keys from his pocket, opened his desk, and took the papers lying there to Downing. After Downing had read them, the spies replaced the papers and re-stored the keys to de Witt's pocket before he awoke.

🎨 **The brush is mightier than the sword.** The Allies in 1944 were girding for the biggest battle in history, the invasion of German-occupied Europe. Across the English Channel, the Germans were throwing up the Atlantic Wall, a formidable system of beach and underwater defenses.

Both sides foresaw a bloodletting. Both sides dreamed of getting hold of the enemy's plans.

Miraculously, the Allies' dream came true.

When the U.S. First Army landed on Utah Beach in France, it was able to pierce the German defenses and push inland. "Securing the blueprint of the German Atlantic Wall was an incredible feat," declared U.S. General Omar Bradley. "So valuable was it that the landing operation succeeded with a minimum loss of men and material."

Who was responsible? A chain of superspies? Not at all.

René Duchez was a house painter-paperhanger by day and member of the French Resistance by night. He was engaged in spiffying up German headquarters in Caen, France, when he noticed a folded map on an officer's desk. It was marked, "Special Blueprint—Top Secret."

The map showed the German defenses in large scale.

While the officer was talking to an aide, Duchez, his heart pounding, snatched the map and slipped it behind a wall mirror. Returning a few days later, he withdrew the map from its hiding place and carried it off, buried among his painting supplies. By the time the Germans missed the copy, it was speeding to London.

The downfall of Adolf Hitler, once a house painter himself, had been hastened by a fellow house painter.

Hat trick. An international congress was being held in Berlin, Germany, in 1878. Although the sessions were secret, Henri Georges Stephan Adolphe Opper de Blowitz, a spy for *The Times* of London, somehow acquired full details of the daily proceedings.

The police shadowed the journalist, but couldn't figure out how he was getting his information. De Blowitz never spoke with anyone connected with the congress.

Nevertheless, de Blowitz *did* have an accomplice, a delegate to the congress. The pair never met.

Each day they dined at the same restaurant at the same hour, but sat far apart. Each put his hat on the hatstand; the hats were similar. When they left, each simply took the other's hat. Packed inside the hat de Blowitz donned was the day's report on the Congress.

Horsing around. More than 2,000 years ago a Roman spy named Cornelius Lelius let several half-trained horses break loose and canter into the enemy camp. Then Lelius sent his "slaves"—actually military officers in disguise—after the horses to bring them back, along with an eyewitness account of the enemy's strength and equipment.

Cane you top this? Drawings of America's hush-hush Norden bombsight were rolled around the stem of an umbrella and smuggled aboard a German ship. A German agent, pretending to limp, used the umbrella as a cane.

When the chips are down. Dusko Popov, a Yugoslav who spied on Allied ships for Germany in Portugal, kept himself posted as to the time and place of each rendezvous by visiting a gambling casino. Another agent placed chips on numbers on a roulette table. The numbers related to the location and time of the next meeting.

"It was an expensive code," admitted Popov.

Stealing bases. A made-to-order cover was that of Morris "Moe" Berg, a major league catcher. In 1934, while barnstorming through Japan with an American all-star baseball team, Berg secretly took films of Tokyo harbor, of warships at anchor, and of fortifications along the shore. Eight years later his films came in handy when the first American air raid on Tokyo was being prepared.

Thanks to Moe Berg, the American flyers scored the military equivalent of a home run.

Words of authority. John Honeyman, whose spying helped George Washington win the Battle of Trenton, feigned loyalty to the British. He played his role so well that his house was attacked by a mob of patriots led by a hotheaded youth of 18, Abraham Baird.

Honeyman was away, but his family was at home. Terrified that the mob would burn the house to the ground, Mrs. Honeyman showed Baird a letter from General Washington.

Above the commander-in-chief's signature Baird read the stern words:

"It is hereby ordered that the wife and children of John Honeyman, of Griggstown, the notorious Tory, now within the British lines, and probably acting the part of a spy, shall be and hereby are protected from all harm and annoyance from any quarter until further notice."

Washington, who doted on his spies, added one more line to keep up the game.

"This furnishes no protection to Honeyman himself."

Shirttale. From 1959 to 1963, Jack Dunlop, an icy-veined spy for the Russians, stole documents from the supersecret U.S. National Security Agency—and calmly strolled out with them tucked under his shirt.

Sharp as a knife. Wat Bowie was a Confederate spy who escaped from a prison in Washington, D.C., and hid in a swampy area of Maryland.

Early one morning he stumbled upon a search party out looking for him. The men had made a fire of wood yanked from a fence and were eating breakfast.

Thinking fast, Bowie chided them, "You're mighty free with my rails. There's all kind of wood around. You don't have to burn my fence."

The men were taken unawares, and Bowie continued his bluff. "Well, after all, war is war. But please don't do any more ruin than is necessary."

"Have you seen Wat Bowie?" one of the men asked, and he described a tall man with brown hair, pug nose,

blue-gray eyes, high forehead, and heavy mustache. The others regarded Bowie sharply—he matched the description.

Bowie's palms began to sweat, but he answered indifferently, "Yes, Wat was around here only last week. They say he went to the far side of Prince George's, where he hails from. I wouldn't know about that."

He stretched lazily and chuckled. "I'm right glad we met here on my land," he said. "Otherwise it might have not been so good for me. Folks say I do resemble him a lot."

And Bowie walked slowly away, making good his escape again.

Entertaining the troops. Attired as a wandering minstrel, King Alfred the Great strummed and sang his way through the Danish army camps. He absorbed enough knowledge of their arms and numbers to defeat the Danes at Edington in the year 878—and today is remembered as the pioneer of the English secret service.

Say it ain't so! At the turn of the nineteenth century, Leonard MacNally, an Irish lawyer, gained the love of his countrymen by defending Irish rebels brought to trial by the British.

Not until after he died did the Irish learn that MacNally had been a spy for the British. He himself had turned in the rebels he so patriotically defended in court.

The good scout. Spies have many different "covers" to protect their identity. Perhaps the most innocent cover was adopted by Robert Baden-Powell, an Englishman. Before World War I he traveled throughout Austria-Hungary posing as a lepidopterist—an authority on butterflies. When not madly chasing the colorful little creatures, he scouted and sketched military installations.

Baden-Powell later became famous for a reason far removed from espionage. He founded the Boy Scouts.

Take my word for it. Alexander Foote, an Englishman who spied in Switzerland for the Russians, had an invisible cover.

He did not appear to be employed or to have any source of income. Whenever friends asked him what he did for a living, Foote blithely answered, "Don't you know? I'm a spy."

No one believed him, a reaction he counted upon.

Not until he published a book about himself after the war did people find out that he had pulled his cover over their eyes. Just as he had said, Alexander Foote had really been a spy.

Drawing interest. Hans Stultz was an instructor at the secret service school in Hamburg, Germany. He taught trainees how to pass for proper Englishmen—to dress, eat, drink, talk, and think like the enemy.

Stultz's lesson on savings banks was his own idea and his masterpiece. The English, he held, were a nation of shopkeepers who looked up to the rich. Hence his students were to put their money in a savings bank. Then they were to go to a police station and claim they had lost their bankbooks. The police, like true working-class Englishmen, judged a man by his bankbook and would be impressed. That kind of groundwork could prove useful.

Most of Stultz's students followed his instructions.

After the visit to the police station, however, they were closely watched.

The spies never guessed that the lost bankbook story was like a calling card announcing their arrival in England. Or that Hans Stultz was a British agent.

Maybe not the champ, but a contender. Two years before the Japanese bombed Pearl Harbor, a German spy had a leisurely, close-up look at American weaponry. He got the innocent Americans to show him around the U.S. arsenal in Maryland by a classic show of sincerity. He had requested a guided tour!

The 140-year-old secret. "Samuel Culper, Jr.," one of George Washington's best spies, kept his identity so secret that not even Washington knew who he really was.

Culper was finally revealed to be Robert Townsend, a Long Island merchant. An historian in the 1930s compared samples of the two men's handwriting and found them identical. Thus Townsend was unmasked more than 140 years after he had retired from espionage.

The check is in the mail. While Benjamin Franklin represented America in Europe during the war, one of his secretaries, Edward Bancroft, was in the pay of the British.

The fact came to light when a bill Bancroft had submitted to the British government for his services was discovered in 1889, more than 100 years later.

Man the washcloth. When Lia de Beaumont was presented at the eighteenth-century Russian court, Empress Elizabeth was so taken with the shy, sweet thing that she appointed Lia a maid of honor. One of Lia's duties was to assist in bathing the elderly ruler.

Little did the empress suspect that the flowing gown, the makeup, and the wig disguised Charles Geneviève Louis Auguste André Timothée d'Eon de Beaumont, a male French spy.

3
The Feminine Touch

Ears looking at you. On the night of December 4, 1777, the British marched out of Philadelphia for a surprise attack on the Continental Army camped at Whitemarsh eight miles away.

The Continentals weren't surprised. Forewarned, they were ready—entrenched and cannon mounted. After a two-day standoff, the British marched back to Philadelphia "like a parcel of fools," having exchanged scarcely a shot.

Four days earlier, British staff officers had entered the home of William and Lydia Darragh and taken over one room for a council chamber. Mrs. Darragh, a wide-awake volunteer spy, had learned of the British attack and managed to get word to the Americans in time.

The British plans had not been gained by some masterstroke—deciphering a code or intercepting a secret message. And, no, the walls did not have ears.

Mrs. Darragh had listened at the keyhole.

Branching out. When Rose Greenhow, the Washington, D.C., society leader and Confederate spy, was arrested, secret service men staked out her house. They waited to nab any of her fellow spies who might stop by.

None fell into the trap.

Greenhow's brash eight-year-old daughter, also named Rose, had climbed a tree next door. To every passerby she knew, she excitedly called down, "Mother has been arrested! Mother has been arrested!"

Little Rose grew up to be an actress.

Hair's looking at you. Betty Duvall, a Confederate agent, carried coded notes in her luxuriant black hair.

Hay, who's reading up there? Elizabeth Van Lew, a Union spy who lived in a mansion in Richmond, Virginia, stayed one step ahead of the enemy.

Despite her high social position, the Confederates searched her home again and again. Wearying of the clumsy raids, she took in boarders, selecting a Confederate officer and his wife. Van Lew sacrificed some of her privacy, but the searches ceased.

Suspicion continued to surround her nonetheless. Van Lew countered by feigning madness. She let her hair fall in uncombed snarls, wore dirty old clothes, and mumbled to herself in public. Soon she became known as "Crazy Lew." Serious concern with the highborn woman's loyalties faded, and she resumed her spying with greater freedom than before. Now, if only she could keep her horse!

The Confederates, critically short of mounts for the army, had ordered that all horses be surrendered. Van Lew needed hers. She often dressed in farmer's home-spun and rode at night to deliver messages to other Union agents outside Richmond. To keep her mount, she stabled him in her upstairs library, having covered the floor with hay. The Confederate officer who lived in the house never was aware of the animal's presence. The horse never snorted, whinnied, or stamped about.

"He was," Van Lew explained, "a very patriotic horse."

 **Knitty-gritty.** Louise de Bettignies, a French spy, was experienced in the art of concealment. She once hid a tiny map of enemy fortifications in the frame of a pair of eyeglasses, and she regularly concealed messages inside balls of knitting wool.

I enjoy being a girl. Belle Boyd was one of the luckiest spies who ever lived. The teenage Confederate sympathizer was jailed, not once but four times, and was always released.

She misfired more often than not. Historians have treated her kindly, glamorizing her hours behind bars. Compared to the romantic glitter of a Boyd in a gilded cage, the glow of success seems but a mere flicker.

For example, the following mishap: Boyd's hometown of Martinsburg, West Virginia, was under Northern control. With military information for the Confederates hot in her hand, she cast about for a means to deliver it. Her eyes fell upon a gentleman in a Confederate uniform. He seemed just the right sort.

Boyd did not pause to wonder why a Confederate was strolling in a Union area free as a jaybird. Perhaps she thought him a paroled prisoner waiting for a ride home.

Whatever her thoughts, she sidled over and in a rapid whisper asked him to deliver a letter for her. He bowed, accepted the sealed envelope graciously, and forthwith turned it over to Union authorities. Boyd was placed under arrest.

The "Confederate" was a Northerner on his way to the South to spy for the North. He did his first job by catching a spy for the South who was spying in the North.

Only Belle Boyd could have starred in such a melodrama—and survived.

Waxworks. Patience Wright, an American sculptor living in London, was the first woman spy for the United States.

Distinguished Britishers who posed in her studio were lulled off guard by her lively charm. While she sculpted them in wax, she picked their brains with seemingly idle chatter that flitted over many subjects —including military and political.

With her studio doubling as an information center, the artful artist was able to forward to America useful tips folded inside wax heads.

Good-bye, Dolly. If she hadn't sent so much mail, Velvalee Dickinson might never have been bagged.

Dickinson owned a doll shop in New York City. She corresponded with clients in many states—and with a Japanese agent in Argentina. The letters to Argentina contained military intelligence disguised as chitchat about dolls. For example, "a doll in a hula skirt" meant that an American warship had arrived from Hawaii.

Dickinson signed the espionage letters with the names of the women clients with whom she conducted harmless business correspondence, and she used their return addresses. The arrangement worked satisfactorily till the Japanese agent left his post and neglected to tell Dickinson.

Like a machine that no one had switched off, she continued sending him letters.

The Argentine post office, unable to locate the addressee, stamped the letters "return to sender." Puzzled women across the United States began to pull returned letters from their mailboxes, letters they had not written.

As all the letters dealt with dolls, and the women had but one place of correspondence in common, the Dickinson Doll Shop in New York City, the trail ended there. The FBI moved in and wrapped up the case.

Hoop-de-do. Jenny Smith was searched and arrested after a Union captain observed her odd and nervous walk. Fastened inside her hoop skirt was a large quantity of highly explosive percussion caps bound for the Confederates.

Hanky-panky. Anna Strong was a patriotic American who lent her wardrobe to the cause.

Her job was to signal another spy when a boatman had arrived to carry messages across the Long Island Sound from New York to Connecticut.

A black petticoat placed on her clothesline indicated that the boatman was waiting. The number of handkerchiefs hung beside it revealed in what cove he was hiding.

The code was foolproof. After all, no one would suspect what Anna's line really was.

Is he or isn't she? The Confederates thought the quiet black man was a slave and put him to work on the fortifications at Yorktown, Virginia. He didn't protest. The labor was hard, but the view was perfect.

The black man made sketches, wadded them into the soles of his shoes, and smuggled them to Union headquarters. The sketches helped General George McClellan capture the town.

The "black man" was neither a slave nor a man, but a soldier named Emma Edmonds. She was not even black; the color was assumed with burnt cork and berry juice. A former nurse, she had enlisted in the army as "Franklin Thompson," later volunteering for dangerous service as a spy. On a few missions she had "posed" as a woman.

Emma Edmonds was the lone female to be accepted as a member of the Grand Army of the Republic, an organization of Union Civil War veterans.

4
Foiling the Foe

Foe-ny order. Americans in Burma came upon a batch of official documents and rubber stamps left behind by the retreating Japanese. Taking advantage of the extraordinary find, they forged a high-command order. It directed a crack Japanese regiment to pull out of the fighting line at once.

The order was entrusted to a Burmese agent working behind enemy lines. In a perfectly timed action, American fighter planes strafed a Japanese staff car, killing the occupants, and the Burmese spy planted the order in the vehicle. Then he told a nearby Japanese unit of the wreck.

The fake order was duly found, and the Japanese obediently withdrew the regiment from the battlefront.

Pipeline. In May, 1942, the Japanese were preparing a major assault in the Central Pacific. Their task fleet consisted of battleships, cruisers, destroyers, aircraft carriers, and submarines. It vastly outnumbered the opposing U.S. fleet.

The Americans had broken the Japanese code and knew the mammoth attack was coming. They did not know *where*. Japanese communications named the target by the letters "AF" only.

What was AF? Some Navy commanders believed it was Oahu in the Hawaiian Islands; others believed it was the Midway Islands. No one was sure, but all agreed our fleet dare not be spread thin. AF had to be pinpointed. In the balance hung the future of the Pacific war.

To solve the mystery, two Naval Intelligence officers, Commanders Joseph Rochefort and E.T. Layton, masterminded an ingenious scheme: Midway radioed naval headquarters at Pearl Harbor that its water distillation plant had broken down. The message was deliberately sent uncoded.

Now, if the Japanese were paying attention . . .

The Americans waited, tense and anxious. After two days of sweating it out, a coded Japanese message was intercepted. It reported that AF was short of drinking water because of a plant breakdown.

AF, then, was *Midway!*

When the Japanese fleet came charging from the northwest, the American fleet was positioned and waiting.

The furious, three-day Battle of Midway climaxed in a smashing Japanese defeat. The victorious Americans moved from the defensive in the Pacific to the offensive, which they held to the end of the war.

Infrared herring. R.V. Jones, a leading English scientist and a celebrated practical joker, combined both talents into a weapon against the enemy.

Through double agents he reached the Germans with news of an amazing invention: an infrared detector that could find submarines traveling under water. The German scientists mounted a crash program to invent an anti-infrared paint. The German Navy began coating its submarines with the stuff.

Jones was full of admiration for the German scientists, especially since his infrared detector was entirely the product of his imagination. It never existed.

Blowing up Britain. Every British citizen, or so it seemed, had an idea for foiling the enemy.

One whopper of a plan called for the construction of a dummy Great Britain. The giant decoy, made of inflated rubber, would be floated in the North Atlantic to bewilder German pilots.

The idea was punctured some distance from the drawing board.

On the beam. R. V. Jones suspected that German aircraft followed radio signals, or beams, that guided them in night bombing runs. The bombers, Jones believed, flew along one beam until they met signals from a second beam. At the intersection, the bombs were released.

Royal Air Force pilots went up and investigated. They found Jones's theory to be correct.

Although it was possible to jam the beams, the practical joker in Jones came up with a better solution. Using a British transmitter, he reproduced one of the German beams. Enemy aircraft were steered off course and off target.

For the next two months, the critical months of September and October, 1940, German bombers wandered around the skies over Britain bombing by guesswork.

Prime Minister Winston Churchill related an instance of German planes unloading more than 100 heavy bombs. All of them exploded in empty fields 10 miles from any town.

Off the beam. For the British bombers flying over Germany, R.V. Jones reversed his trick with the radio beams. He aimed beams (which he named J beams) over Germany, and made sure the enemy learned about them.

The Germans jammed the J beams, but without effect—the British planes were actually guiding themselves by radar. After six months, the Germans discovered they had been duped and ignored the J beams.

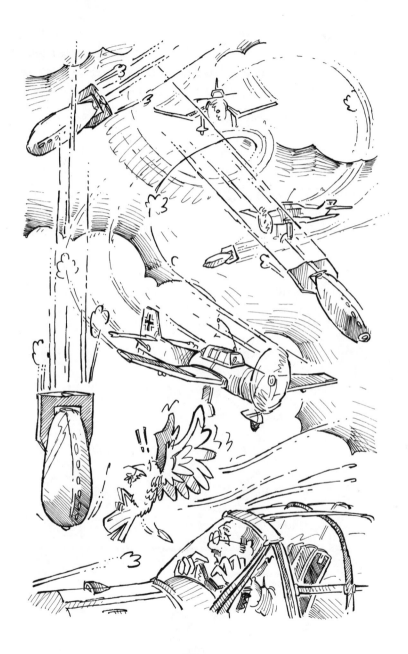

At that point, the British bombers switched over from radar and followed the J beams to their targets. The Germans, outfoxed once, did not bother to jam the beams anymore, being convinced the beams were a decoy!

 **Drink to me only with thine eyes.** Before the invasion of Europe on June 6, 1944, the Allies tried all kinds of ways to mislead the Germans about their landing points. A dandy sideshow of a scheme called for someone to impersonate British Field Marshal Bernard Montgomery.

Tapped for the role was British Lieutenant Meyrick James, a former actor. He bore a striking resemblance to Montgomery.

For weeks James was trained in Montgomery's gestures, walk, bearing, personality, and manner of speaking. Then he was flown to Gibraltar and North Africa, where he plunged into rounds of meetings and receptions. The German spies were meant to think he was organizing a major operation against southern France.

But the scenario hit a snag. Montgomery loathed liquor and tobacco. James loved both. Rumors reached London that "Montgomery" had been seen weaving drunkenly around Algiers while puffing a big black cigar.

The project went up in smoke and had to be scotched. James was recalled to London.

Give me some men . . . In the winter of 1777, General Washington and his army were encamped at Morristown, New Jersey. Washington had only 4,000 troops. To forestall an attack, he wanted the British to think he had far more.

So he spread a rumor that he had an army of 24,000. He scattered his ragtag men in houses throughout the town, creating the illusion of great numbers.

A British spy posing as a merchant arrived in camp. Instead of arresting him, the Americans pretended to befriend him. They arranged to let him steal a peek at touched-up documents that gave "proof" of a huge American army in Morristown.

The British were convinced. Then a British intelligence officer, American-born William Luce, discovered the true number. Luce had been taken prisoner, but was paroled. He used the opportunity to study the American troops at Morristown, and when he had collected accurate information, broke his parole and fled to British headquarters in New York.

Much to his horror, he was not believed. The British, who already had the "true" figures from the first spy, thought Luce was trying to deceive them. General Sir William Howe threatened to hang him "from the first tree," but eventually was content to dismiss him with contempt.

The army that wasn't. The "First United States Army Group," known as FUSAG, dwarfed all other hoaxes in history for ambition and scope. The Germans fell for it.

FUSAG was a mixture of manpower and equipment, part real and part unreal. The real army in the group was to land in Normandy, France, in support of the Allied invasion.

The phantom army was to stay behind in England, worrying the Germans with the threat of a second Allied invasion. It had trucks, guns, planes, and tanks— made of canvas, plywood, papier-mâché, chicken wire, and inflated rubber. A movie studio manufactured false docks along with false landing craft that spewed smoke from their funnels. No mock-up had ever been assembled on so grand a scale.

The crowning touch was FUSAG's commander, George S. Patton, Jr. A swashbuckling tank genius, Patton was the general whom the Germans most feared.

When neither FUSAG nor Patton reinforced the Allied beachheads, the Germans uneasily bided their time. Expecting Patton to lead a follow-up invasion at some other point on the continent, they held back 19 divisions until it was too late.

Tens of thousands of German soldiers—soldiers who might have thrown the Allied troops into the sea—were sidelined by the magnificent hoax.

Dropouts. One night in the middle of 1940, two German spies parachuted into England. Within weeks, at least 25 more agents dropped from the skies. Still more followed by sea and air.

The influx of daring men and women, most of them in their twenties, was the advance guard in Germany's plan to bomb England into surrendering. It was their job to secure detailed information on British antiaircraft positions, troop concentrations, and hidden hangars and airfields.

Reports were slow in coming. When at last radio messages began crackling from England to Germany, the spearhead of spies was hailed as a roaring success.

The triumphant Germans never suspected the truth. Their spies had met with disaster. The British had captured every last one.

Those spies who refused to cooperate were jailed or executed. Those who chose to cooperate took part in the hoax as the mouthpieces of their captors.

The Germans went on happily receiving all that military information—and every word was what the British wanted them to receive.

Can't keep a secret. During the first years of the war the Allies picked out German factories from aerial photographs with amazing ease. Why? Because the Germans doused camouflage paint only over factories making armaments. Factories not producing war materials were left uncamouflaged.

Instead of hiding their war plants, the Germans unintentionally presented the Allies with an easy way to recognize them.

Body language. The Allies had conquered North Africa and were girding to move north against the island of Sicily. To misguide the enemy, they enlisted the services of a dead man.

Dressed in a British uniform and provided with identification tags and other items, the corpse became "Acting Major William Martin, 09560, Royal Marines, a staff officer at Combined Operations Headquarters." The addition of personal possessions, including a partly smoked pack of cigarettes, a box of matches, a bill for a diamond engagement ring, two bus tickets, coins and paper money, and a pair of theater tickets completed the rebirth.

In a leather briefcase chained to Major Martin's wrist were papers revealing that the Allies intended to invade Sardinia and two Greek islands in the eastern Mediterranean, with a feint toward western Sicily.

The body was laid in a metal cylinder packed with dry ice and taken aboard a British submarine. At 4:15 A.M. on April 30, 1943, the body was removed from the cylinder, fitted in to a Mae West life jacket, and dropped overboard off the coast of Spain. Now it was all up to Major Martin. He must float to shore and be found by the Spanish, who must think he had been killed in a plane crash at sea.

The ruse worked. Each step ticked off with exquisite success. The body was discovered. The "official" papers were copied, and the copies relayed to German intelligence. The Germans studied every paper, every personal possession. The verdict, as scribbled in German on one of Major Martin's letters, was unanimous: "The genuineness of the captured documents is above suspicion."

The Germans made ready for the invasion they "knew" was coming. They marshaled their forces in Sardinia, Greece, and western Sicily. On July 9, 1943, the Allies landed on the beaches of southern Sicily. The enemy had been led astray by a corpse.

Going Greta one better. He was a dashing Spaniard who used the code name "Garbo"—a name made famous by actress Greta Garbo, who wanted to be alone. It was fitting. He staged a one-man spy show with nothing but his cunning and an imaginary supporting cast.

With the patter of a born showman, he convinced the German embassy in Madrid, Spain, of his worth as a spy. The Germans, whom he hated, outfitted him with funds, forged papers, and invisible ink.

Off he went, avowedly to London. Instead, he set up shop in Lisbon, Portugal. From there he fed the Germans phony but believable espionage reports supposedly coming from England.

Earlier, when Garbo had volunteered his services to British intelligence, he had been brushed off. So successful did his free-lance operation become that now they sought his aid and whisked him to England.

While in Lisbon, Garbo had created three "subagents." In England, his mythical network grew to 14 "agents" and 11 well-placed "contacts." His "organization" sent 400 letters and 2,000 radio messages to the Germans, who continued to trust him.

The British valued Garbo's work highly enough to award him the prized Order of the British Empire. And just about the same time, he received another honor—the Iron Cross from the grateful Germans!

Hans off. He might someday be extremely useful, and so the Germans put up with him. His name was Hans Hansen, and he radioed reports from England.

Like ordinary folk, he could be lazy, vain, greedy, and dense.

Sometimes he would radio that he didn't feel like spying for a while. He was taking a vacation.

Once he complained bitterly: "You never let me know what you think of my work. An occasional pat on the back would be welcome. After all, I am only human."

When some money he was expecting didn't arrive, he fumed: "What is delaying the man with the money you promised? I am beginning to think you are full of dirt."

The Germans urgently wanted information on bread in England in order to judge shortages. Hansen responded to the inquiry: "Don't you have anything more important to ask? The bread tastes all right."

The Germans tore their hair, but endured his complaints and his insults. What they didn't know was that he had been captured and was now being controlled by the British.

Deceiving the deceivers. Even while the British were fooling them with the Double-Cross Committee, the Germans had a similar operation of their own. In 1942, their counterespionage agents in the German-occupied Netherlands arrested Hubert Lauwers a Dutch radio operator. Lauwers had been working for the British.

To save his life, Lauwers agreed to continue communicating with the British, but with the Germans at his shoulder. On the strength of Lauwers's messages, the British parachuted agents and supplies into the

Netherlands. By the time the British learned they had been duped, the Germans had rounded up more than 50 agents, thousands of weapons, and immense quantities of explosives.

The deceived deceived the deceivers. Each side was fooling the other in a deadly game of foxes. Each side was busily sending its agents into the arms of the enemy.

X-ing out the enemy. Wrong information is sometimes as important as true information in espionage. Wrong information is called "disinformation."

Thanks to disinformation sent to Germany by agents the British had captured, the Germans expected attacks by armies that didn't exist, told their submarines to avoid minefields that were fictional, and directed their V rockets and bombs to where they did no damage.

The British command group that handled captured spies who "turned" against Germany had a well-chosen name. It was the XX Committee—the Double-Cross Committee.

Herrmail. One of the cleverest Allied tricks succeeded not only in feeding the Germans propaganda, but made them swallow it.

Each side had grown accustomed to propaganda coming via the radio or in leaflets from the sky. Such news and views had less and less effect. But what if messages came by a trusted carrier—say, the neighborhood postman?

Letters written in England and addressed to real Germans were stuffed into mailbags. Allied fighter-bombers then blasted German trains carrying mail, and the mailbags were dropped amid the wreckage.

German salvage crews did the rest. All the mailbags, both bogus and genuine, were collected and in due course distributed through the postal system.

Because the propaganda reached German breakfast tables, the Allies called their brainchild "Operation Cornflakes."

5
Sending Messages and Breaking Codes

Amateur night. The Americans hired a local daredevil. His task was to destroy the new electric coding machine in the German embassy of a neutral country.

The man was long on courage, but short on understanding modern machinery. So the chief of the Office of Strategic Services (O.S.S.) whittled the mission to the bone: Blow up the most complicated machine in the embassy coding room.

The man sneaked by the guards and set off a charge, narrowly saving his own life in the explosion. The next day the Americans were flabbergasted. The Germans continued to send out machine-coded messages.

The daredevil had blown up the electric coffee maker!

A medal is a medal. An American detachment behind Japanese lines in Burma sent a coded message late in 1943. In a request for supplies were the letters "CMA," which baffled the receiving operator. He decided that CMA stood for "Citation for Military Assistance."

Accordingly, 50 medals were cast in silver and strung on gaudy silk ribbons. The medals bore the letters "CMA" above an American eagle.

When the decorations arrived in Burma, they were distributed among the hardy Burmese rangers assisting the Americans. The pleased rangers wore the cherished citation, happily ignorant of the truth: CMA was short for "comma."

Spy baby. A French dwarf named Richeberg was probably the youngest and smallest "spy" ever. When he was an infant, 23 inches tall, Royalists during the French Revolution used him to carry dispatches in and out of Paris. The papers were concealed in Richeberg's baby clothes.

Tom-tom talk. All the complicated electronic code machines of the armies, navies, and air forces could not match the system used by the U.S. Marines in the South Pacific. They recruited Navajo Indians to man combat radios.

Navajos talked to Navajos, and no Japanese was able to understand what they were saying. The Navajo language was an unbreakable code.

🪂 **Thanks anyway.** Without clearing it first with Washington, O.S.S. agents raided the Japanese embassy in Lisbon, Portugal, and seized a code book. They thought they had scored a coup.

Unknown to the agents, U.S. cryptologists had already solved the code and were able to read Japanese communications—until the raid on the embassy. The Japanese immediately changed their code worldwide, and it was more than a year before the U.S. cracked the new one.

🪂 **Flash on the barrelhead.** A knotty problem faced two American agents in France: how to disguise their mobile transmitter so that the Germans would not locate it.

To foil the enemy's directional finders, the two Americans dug deep into their bag of tricks. They came up with a large hogshead, or cask, of the type favored by local wine peddlers. The cask was customized with boards in the middle. Inside the bottom half was wine. Inside the top half one of the agents curled up with the radio transmitter.

While the agent inside sent messages, his partner, garbed as a peddler, pushed the hogshead down the street. If a customer asked for wine, the "peddler" obliged by removing the bung from the lower half and letting the wine flow.

Should a German directional-finding truck approach, the man outside stopped pushing, the signal for the man inside to stop sending.

Anything from the hippopotamus yet? Agents of a French spy network in occupied France used the names of animals as cover names. The network became known, naturally, as "Noah's Ark."

Bellyful. During the Thirty Years' War, a courier made it through the lines at the siege of Arras, France, in 1634, with a message encased in lead and sunk in his stomach.

Separating de friends from de foe. Secret agent Daniel Defoe was traveling around England in 1720 under the name Alexander Goldsmith. One town Defoe was to visit was Weymouth. He told his chief to forward messages there in care of a Captain Turner.

By ill chance, there were two Captain Turners living in the town, and the wrong one got a letter meant for Defoe. Finding that it was written in code, the captain exhibited it around town, to the excitement of all. A spy lurked in their midst! The townsfolk organized a manhunt. Defoe barely managed to escape with his skin—and to write *Robinson Crusoe*.

Whatever befell Defoe's Captain Turner is not recorded.

Tap, tap, who's there? A Union officer of the young Army Signal Corps spliced into a Confederate wire below Washington, D.C. He eavesdropped long enough to learn the names of a few Confederate units. Then he tapped out orders designed to bait them into an ambush.

The Confederates didn't bite. They instantly recognized a newcomer by his unfamiliar touch and tapped back: "We know you're there . . . get off our line, you damn yankee!"

Button, button. Confederate agents reduced messages photographically and hid them inside metal buttons sewed onto coats. The technique was the forerunner of the microphotography used by today's spies.

Their civic duty. United States propaganda leaflets aimed at the police were dropped over Japan. Printed boldly at the top of the leaflets were the following words in Japanese:

"Warning. This is an enemy publication. The finder is commanded to take this to the nearest police station immediately."

Good citizens obeyed and brought the leaflets to the police. The propaganda scored a bull's-eye.

The better way. Since mail could be sent from England to Germany by way of neutral countries, German agent Jules Silber bypassed the hugger-mugger of other spies. His knowledge of languages landed him a job in the postal censorship section of British Military Intelligence, and he stamped his envelopes "Passed by the Censor."

Getting the bugs out. Now and then the Allies picked up down-to-earth radio directions from Hermann Göring, Germany's Air Force chief. Göring reminded his officers to make sure that airmen to whom he was going to award medals were deloused before he decorated them.

Enough to drive you crazy. American soldiers overseas were forbidden to mention the place where they were stationed. One GI thought he could outwit the censor.

Before being shipped out, he told his family that he would let them know where he was by placing a different middle initial in his father's name on each letter. The initials would spell out his location.

In five successive letters the soldier spelled out T-U-N-I-S. He received an inquiry from his family. His letters had not arrived in the proper order, and he had not dated them. As far as his puzzled family could tell, the soldier was in a place called N-U-T-S-I.

For another dollar he could have wired flowers. American security before the attack on Pearl Harbor was woefully lax.

The evening of December 6, 1941, as the Japanese fleet was drawing near, Takeo Yoshikawa, a Japanese spy, coded a message. He described the American warships anchored at the naval base and observed "It appears that no air reconnaissance is being conducted by the fleet air arm."

At 6:01 P.M., Yoshikawa walked right up to the counter in the RCA Radiogram office in Pearl Harbor and sent the historic message. It cost him $6.82.

Once more from the bottom. Although he was untrained in coding, a Union telegrapher altered a telegram from President Lincoln so that only a keen head could understand it.

CITY POINT, VA., 8:30 A.M. APRIL 3, 1865 TINKER, WAR DEPARTMENT: A LINCOLN ITS IN FUME A IN HYMN TO START I ARMY TREATING THERE POSSIBLE IF OF CUT TOO FORWARD PUSHING IS HE SO ALL RICHMOND AUNT CON-

FIDE IS ANDY EVACUATED PETERSBURG REPORTS GRANT
MORNING THIS WASHINGTON SECRETARY WAR.

To understand the message, read it rapidly—and
backward.

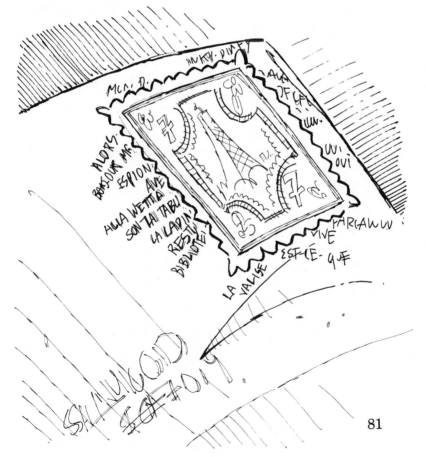 **A picture is worth 1,600 words.** Paul Bernard, a
French mapmaker and spy, could write a 1,600-word
report on a postcard within the space allotted to a
stamp. When the stamp was pasted on, the report was
completely covered.

What's a four-letter word for D-day? The Germans should have worked the crossword puzzles in London's *Daily Telegraph*. Shortly before the invasion of Normandy, the puzzles included five of the ultrasecret code names used in the D-day landings: Mulberry (floating docks); Omaha and Utah (beachheads); Neptune (naval phase); and Overlord (overall).

Leonard Dawe and Melville Jones had composed the puzzles. They were able to prove their innocence to the wildly anxious spy catchers who visited and revisited them: the puzzles were made up months in advance. The code names were a coincidence, an utterly fantastic, nerve-racking coincidence.

Special delivery. About 500 B.C., Histiaeus, the ruler of Miletus, resolved to break away from the Persian empire. Histiaeus was then visiting the Persian court; his loyal follower, Aristagoras, governed Miletus in his stead.

Since his rooms were guarded, Histiaeus racked his brains for a method of getting word to Aristagoras. He could think of no safer way than to write the order to rebel in headlines.

Histiaeus shaved all the hair from the head of his most trusted slave. Upon the naked scalp he wrote his message and waited till the hair grew back.

Then he sent off the slave with the simplest of instructions: "Bid Aristagoras shave your head and look at it."

6
Offbeat Espionage

Playing the heavy. Parachuting agents into enemy territory was seldom a breeze. Occasionally men and women became airsick. Sometimes it required a shove from behind to overcome fright.

One German had a weightier problem: He was too fat. He lowered himself into the small hole cut in the fuselage of the plane. To his horror he became as stuck as a plug. He squirmed frantically, his legs flapping in the wind currents under the plane.

Crew members stomped on the luckless fellow till they pushed him through the hole.

Play it again, Uncle Sam. President Franklin D. Roosevelt and British Prime Minister Winston Churchill were slated to meet in mid-January, 1943. The Ger-

mans desperately wanted to find out where. An all-out espionage campaign correctly fixed on "Casablanca."

But that was too simple for the shrewd minds in German intelligence. Casablanca had to be a code name. Didn't *casa blanca* mean "white house" in Spanish?

While the Germans concentrated on the White House in Washington, D.C., Roosevelt and Churchill met thousands of miles away in Casablanca, Morocco.

Know how. The Carthaginian general Hannibal made ingenious use of enemy spies.

One afternoon it came to his attention that several of his soldiers had deserted to the Romans the previous night, and that Roman spies were in his camp. Hannibal strode through his army thundering his anger. The name "deserter" should not be applied to his bravest soldiers, who, at his order, had gone out to learn the enemy's plans.

As soon as the Roman spies heard his words, they raced back to their lines. The deserters were seized and returned to Hannibal considerably worse for wear.

Hello, Jell-O . Americans Harry Gold and David Greenglass were both involved in stealing the atomic bomb secrets for Russia. To identify themselves to each other at their first meeting, they held up matching pieces torn from a box of Jell-O.

The two eventually received their just desserts.

I'm me, who's ewe? Admiral Wilhelm Canaris, chief of Abwehr, the German secret service, mistrusted friend and foe.

One day Canaris was driving down a country road in Spain with a fellow officer. All at once Canaris stopped the car, jumped out, and snapped a military salute to a shepherd tending a flock of sheep by the side of the road.

"You can never tell when there's a senior officer underneath," Canaris explained to his dumbfounded companion.

Frustration special. Thomas Conrad was a Confederate spy in the right place at the right time, but . . .

Conrad paced the streets of the enemy's capital, Washington, D.C., as Union troops rushed off to the Battle of Gettysburg. The city was being stripped of manpower, leaving most of its defenses in the hands of panicky civilians.

Watching the bluecoats depart, Conrad had the thrilling sense of balancing destiny. A sizeable, combat-hardened Confederate force could brush aside the amateur defenders, take the Union capital, and perhaps even capture President Lincoln. The opportunity was dazzling.

Conrad galloped out of Washington in search of Confederate General J.E.B. "Jeb" Stuart, who was nearby. The perfect man for the mission, the fast-moving cavalry commander was renowned for his lightning strikes. But so fast-moving was Stuart that Conrad couldn't overtake him. Washington was saved, never to be endangered again.

Informed of the lost chance, Stuart lamented, "I would have charged down Pennsylvania Avenue!"— and changed the history of the war.

Not sew smart. German spies sent into Russia wore copies of Russian uniforms. In tailoring them, the thorough Germans outdid themselves. They sewed the shoulder tabs neatly onto the sleeves, whereas the Russians carelessly let the tabs hang loose.

The stitching was a minor error, but a fatal one.

Name that spy. The names of high officials in the British Secret Intelligence, MI-6, are tightly guarded. So the public was shocked when a German official, in a most ungentlemanly way, named all the chiefs in a public speech.

With typical British self-possession, the service marked its copy of the speech "Most Secret"—and went on with its work as if nothing had happened.

Identity problem. Ignaz Trebitsch—who later became Ignatius Timothy Trebitsch Lincoln—was born into the Jewish faith and studied to be a rabbi. He became an Anglican and then a Lutheran. He returned to Anglicanism and was ordained a deacon. He then became a Buddhist.

A Hungarian who took British citizenship, Trebitsch worked for a businessman, was elected to Parliament, turned to journalism, and became a spy. He sold Bulgarian secrets to Turkey and Turkish secrets to the Bulgarians, and all the while he was spying for Germany too. He wound up in China as a secret agent of the government.

When he died there in 1943, Ignaz Trebitsch had become the Abbot Chao Kung.

Home sweet Holmes. Special Operations Executive, the undercover agency that governed British spies in German-occupied Europe, had its headquarters on London's Baker Street. The ghost of Sherlock Holmes must have approved. Holmes "lived" on the same street during his years as fiction's master detective.

Strike up the band. The Red Orchestra was a web of Russian spies that extended throughout most of Europe. Agents of the orchestra were called "violinists."

The Black Orchestra was a group of German officers that plotted to overthrow Adolf Hitler before and during the war.

Although neither orchestra ever produced a sound of music, members knew that if they ever dropped a note they could swing.

Look, C the chief. The chiefs of MI-6, the British intelligence service, have always been known as "C."

The first chief of MI-6 was Mansfield Smith-Cumming, a one-legged naval officer who wore a gold-rimmed monocle and wrote in green ink. Smith-Cumming felt his identity should be secret, and he chose as his code designation the letter C—the initial of his second surname.

C grew into a tradition. Since Smith-Cumming, all MI-6 chiefs have been C.

Slighted. Benjamin Franklin Stringfellow became one of the Confederacy's most daring spies. But when he tried to enlist in the Army at the start of the war, he was rejected because he was too slight. He weighed less than 100 pounds.

Hold the pretzels. The Germans waited expectantly for the first radio message from a newly recruited spy, a Welshman.

"Here he comes!" blurted the radio operator.

The message came through loud and clear: "Ein Glas Bier!"—"A glass of beer!"

Those were the only German words the Welshman knew.

A stable spy. A young agent of the Mossad, Israel's intelligence service, journeyed to Cairo, Egypt, as a tourist. He was to ascertain what kind of cover was best to use when he returned there to live.

The agent visited a horse-breeding farm run by Wolfgang Lotz, who was rumored to be a former Nazi. The agent was impressed by the number of Egyptian officers that came to the farm. He concluded that a similar operation would be a fruitful source of intelligence.

Back in Israel he proposed the idea.

"Why not let me open a horse farm like that fascist swine Wolfgang Lotz?" he said eagerly. "I paid one visit to the place, and it's crawling with Egyptian Army men who have nothing better to do than ride that Nazi's horses. I'll set up another riding school. When I get friendly with Lotz, I'll finish him off. What do you think?"

His idea was politely rejected without explanation.

Wolfgang Lotz was an ace Israeli spy posing as an ex-Nazi. His horse farm was paid for by the Mossad, and the service didn't care to run *two* such costly operations in Egypt.

All for espionage. During the reign of Queen Elizabeth I of England spies faced dangers unheard of today.

A German named Wychegerde spied for Elizabeth in Spain. His profession as a traveling merchant in grain and sundries lent him a natural cover.

On one trip the cover boomeranged. He fell into the clutches of pirates, who relieved him of all his wares, the last coin in his pockets, and even his clothing. He was freed in France, wearing nothing but his underwear! His information was naturally a little skimpy.

You are what you eat. As Daniel Taylor was being hustled off for questioning, he shoved a shiny object into his mouth and gulped it down. He wasn't fast enough to escape notice. His captors forced a dose of "'tartar emetic" down his throat.

Taylor vomited. Up came a hollow silver ball about the size of a rifle bullet. Inside was a brief message for the British.

As an American general is said to have commented, "Out of thine own mouth shalt thou be condemned."

What can you get for a nickel these days? One evening in 1953 a newspaper delivery boy was collecting money from his customers in an apartment building in Brooklyn, New York. A lady came to the door. She fetched her purse, looked inside, and said, "Sorry, Jimmy, I don't have any change. Can you break this dollar bill for me?"

The youngster counted the coins in his pocket and shook his head. "I'll try the people across the hall," he said. He got change from two ladies in another apartment.

As he was leaving the building, he noticed that one of the coins in his hand, a nickel, seemed peculiar. He rested it on his middle finger. It felt lighter than an ordinary nickel.

He dropped the coin on the floor. It fell apart. Inside it the boy found a tiny photograph of what appeared to be a series of numbers.

Two days later the FBI heard about the strange coin. The subject had arisen during a conversation between a New York detective and another police officer, whose daughter was friendly with the newsboy. The detective told the FBI.

FBI agents examined the coin. The numbers in the photograph appeared to be a code of some kind. . . .

The ensuing FBI investigation stretched across the United States. Four years later, the net fell on a man calling himself "Emil R. Goldfus." He finally confessed himself to be Rudolph Ivanovich Abel, a colonel in Russian intelligence. Under the cover of a painter-photographer, Abel had directed the Russian spy legions in the U.S. for 10 years.

The long and tangled paths that led to Abel, one of Russia's most valued spies, had begun with a hollow nickel in the hand of a curious Brooklyn newspaper boy.

A barbarous notion. In the early 1960s the C.I.A., successor to the Office of Strategic Services (O.S.S.), considered a plot to inject Cuban dictator Fidel Castro with a chemical that would make his beard fall off.

The high cost of freedom. George Washington spent a total of $17,617 on espionage activities during the entire American Revolution.

The United States, in order to protect itself, today spends more dollars than that on espionage every five minutes of every day of the year.

That's $pying!

Plumb accurate. Before hitting Makin Island in the Pacific, the Americans estimated the strength of the Japanese garrison at 4,000 men. They were right to within 40 men.

The credit belonged to an interpreter of aerial photographs. He counted latrines. Then he multiplied by the regular Japanese Army ratio of latrines to men.

The legend of Albert Oertel. The story was first reported in the *Saturday Evening Post* magazine. It was repeated in the memoirs of Walter Schellenberg, who had headed German intelligence. The director of the U.S. Central Intelligence Agency, Allen Dulles, told it to a graduating class of agents.

In 1927 Albert Oertel, a German naval officer in the First World War, moved to Great Britain but kept his contact with German naval intelligence. He established himself as a jeweler and watchmaker in a shop on the Orkney Islands, not far from the main anchorage of the British Home Fleet at Scapa Flow.

Shortly after the outbreak of World War II in 1939, Oertel advised the Germans that no boom and no adequate anti-submarine nets blocked the eastern approach to Scapa Flow. Armed with these tidings, a German submarine entered the sea basin and sank the British aircraft carrier *Royal Oak*. Oertel drove at high speed along the shore, signaling the submarine with his headlight.

A fine story, often retold, except that later research showed that no such person as Albert Oertel ever existed!

Nevertheless, *someone* was seen driving with one headlight on—despite the blackout regulations—just before the sinking. For nearly forty years no one knew who that somone was.

Royal Oak's killer was the German submarine *U-47*, which sailed for Scapa Flow from Kiel on the morning of October 8, 1939, the sixth Sunday of World War II. In command was Captain-Lieutenant Günther Prien, a young skipper handpicked for the operation by Commodore Karl Dönitz, commander of Germany's U-boat warfare.

Even though Scapa Flow was an easy target, many in Prien's crew felt they would never survive the dangerous mission. During the First World War, two U-boats had been lost in similar raids.

Shortly before midnight of Friday, October 13, *U-47* entered Scapa Flow on a tricky, following tide. The sea was high and calm, the night fairly clear. The submarine ran above the surface.

As *U-47* made her way through the narrow eastern passage of Kirk Sound, she passed the village of St. Mary's. Men on the bridge were startled by the sudden appearance of a car. It came around a far corner of the village and stopped opposite the submarine, its one headlight pointing like a searchlight. Presently the driver turned off the headlight and went racing along the shore road toward the town of Kirkwall.

Lt. Prien thought he had been spotted and that destroyers would hunt him down. Nonetheless, he continued on. In the northeast corner of the anchorage he found two "fat fellows." He fired, and one of the torpedoes struck *Royal Oak*. The 620-foot warship withstood the blow, remaining afloat despite a 50-foot gash in her starboard bow.

After cruising around for 12 minutes, Lt. Prien returned for a second attack. He scored hits with three torpedoes, and these were fatal. *Royal Oak* sank at 1:30 A.M., October 14, taking with her 833 officers and men. Lt. Prien retraced his entrance route through Kirk

Sound and escaped from Scapa Flow without being discovered. A true hero, he was lionized in his homeland.

And the mystery car?

While *U-47* was ghosting into Scapa Flow on electric motors, Robbie Tullock, a taxi driver, was looking forward to bed after a busy night.

As he was making his way home, two young men who worked at the nearby Royal Hotel hailed him. They wanted to be taken to the dance at the Drill Hall in St. Mary's. Tullock refused. It was nearly midnight. He had a fare scheduled for six in the morning, and he needed sleep. The two men pleaded so earnestly that he finally agreed to take them. On the way he stopped at the Royal Hotel to pick up two young women who also wanted to attend the dance.

Arriving at the Drill Hall, Tullock heard music from inside. By the door stood three soldiers. They were chatting with a circle of young women, breaking off only to close the blackout curtain when someone went in or out of the hall.

The soldiers carried rifles with bayonets fixed. Tullock wondered why they needed the weapons while on such casual duty.

After he had dropped off his passengers, Tullock turned around and drove down the slope to the bottom of Hill Road. There he stopped by the post office. He was facing Kirk Sound. The taxi's one working headlight, which was masked, shone on the water.

It occurred to Tullock that the night was ideal for an enemy submarine to slip into Scapa Flow.

After a while he switched off the headlight as he

could see well enough without it. He turned right onto the shore road and drove home at full speed, using his sidelights only.

The next morning he learned of the sinking of *Royal Oak*. He recalled the three armed soldiers at the dance. Incorrectly he concluded that their real duty was to keep a lookout for enemy craft. He reasoned that if he came forward and told what he had seen—that the soldiers had been flirting while on guard—they would be court-martialed and perhaps shot.

So he held his tongue for nearly forty years.

Not until he was convinced that no one would be harmed by his story did he burst the legend of the mystery car.

A taxi driver was merely dousing his headlight, the better to observe the blackout regulations along the coast.

Coming on strong. The Japanese, who dread disgrace—what they call "loss of face"—were naturals for a bit of American mischief.

The Research and Development Division of the O.S.S. cooked up a foul-smelling goo and nicknamed it "Who Me?" Applied to clothing, Who Me? was almost impossible to scrub away. Soft tubes filled with the stuff were dealt out to boys in Chinese cities occupied by the Japanese.

The boys waited for a Japanese officer to stroll down the street. Darting behind him, they sprayed his trousers with the long-lasting stink.

While the officer reddened in humiliation, the boys raced for safety, having caused a loss of face with a squirt on the seat.

And that, naturally, marks The End.

ABOUT THE AUTHOR

For more than a decade, DONALD J. SOBOL has been engaged in research for a work on the history of spying. "I discovered early," he says, "that not all spies were romantic, successful, and clever. Some were outright bumblers. Even a few major wartime intelligence projects turned wacky side up. The odd and funny incidents of espionage kept prodding me for their own book. So here it is."

Mr. Sobol is the author of the highly acclaimed Encyclopedia Brown books. His awards for these books include the Pacific Northwest Reader's Choice Award for *Encyclopedia Brown Keeps the Peace* and a special Edgar from the Mystery Writers of America for his contribution to mystery writing in the United States.

Donald Sobol is married and has three children. A native of New York, he now lives in Florida.